MW61177817

CONSCIOUS MOMENT

FINDING PEACE AMID THE DIN

LUCY COSTIGAN

ENLIGHTEN PUBLISHING

DEDICATION

In memory of my dear cousin, Raymond J. McGovern,
in love and light always.

Conscious Moment:
Finding Peace Amid The Din

All Rights Reserved © 2020 by Lucy Costigan

Published 2020
By Enlighten Publishing,
14 Thomas Street,
Wexford,
Ireland

This is a new, revised and updated version of a previously published work, entitled 'Course in Consciousness', by Lucy Costigan, published by iUniverse, Inc., NE, USA, in 2004.

www.enlightenpublishing.com

Email: info@enlightenpublishing.com

ISBN: 978-0-9930188-2-4

Cover photo: Selective focus photography of leaves with water drop, courtesy of www.Pexels.com.

Cover design: Michael Cullen of IrishImages.Org.

ACKNOWLEDGEMENTS

Thanks to my editors, Tony Walsh and Theresa Cullen, for their constructive comments that have greatly enhanced the clarity of the final version of this book.

Thanks to my family and friends who support me on a daily basis: Tony for your love and support; Anthony, Kathleen, Sharon and Martin, Lisa, Antoinette and Aidan; Theresa, Sean, Michael, Paul, Damien and Hilda; Val and Yvonne; Geraldine McGovern, my dear cousin; Isabel MacMahon, Clara Martin, Maura O'Connor, Carmel Larkin, Rita and Jimmy Murphy.

Thanks also to my dear cousin, Geraldine McGovern, for sharing so much of her journey, her deep wisdom and her loving heart.

In memory of Kila, Lynsey and Sophie Ruby, my dearest companions and wisest teachers for many wonderful years.

ABOUT THE AUTHOR

Lucy Costigan is an Irish author. 'Strangest Genius: The Stained Glass of Harry Clarke', (with photographer Michael Cullen), was shortlisted for Best Irish-Published Book in 2010 by the Irish Book Awards, and for Book of the Decade by Dublin Book Festival in 2016. In 2012, Lucy's biography, 'Glenveagh Mystery' about the Harvard professor, Arthur Kingsley Porter, who mysteriously disappeared from Co. Donegal in 1933, became a national bestseller. Lucy's working life has been quite eclectic and includes careers in technical writing, counselling and social care. She holds Master's Degrees in Research and Equality Studies. Lucy lives in Wexford Town with her partner, Tony, and their border collie, Ivan.

CONTENTS

INTRODUCTION

Our world is a miraculous place, yet life in the twenty-first century has become ultra-busy, fast and noisy. Commercialism and consumerism engulf us, ensuring that many children are reared to admire and crave a surface reality. In schools and workplaces, competition is advocated far more than co-operation. The failure of our social institutions to provide fair and transparent leadership–particularly in the areas of church, state and finance, and the subsequent exposure of grave abuses within these systems–has led to general disgust, mistrust and apathy. As religious beliefs and practices begin to wane, and ethics and philosophy are not included in general education, there exists a void in our spiritual and emotional development.

Yet every soul still requires nourishment, lots of space and a little quietness before it can open its fountain of wisdom. We can enjoy all the gifts that this physical world has to offer, yet to live at a surface level and never to explore all the multi-dimensions that lie within, would truly be a lost opportunity for soulful living for the time we spend on earth. At the core of our being there is infinite love, awareness and joy. Our task is to learn how to open to our soul's wisdom, to awaken, and to revel in our light-filled, joyful nature.

Developing awareness is not only for gurus or avatars. Awareness or consciousness is an integral part of all of us, the very fabric of our being, yet we must learn how to open to this dimension. You may have experienced a moment when something shifted deep within, and you absolutely knew which step you needed to take, or the truth of some profound insight that had suddenly emerged. In one moment there may appear a profound insight that clarifies some problem that was giving you sleepless nights, or you experience a gut feeling that gives you the courage to move forward on your unique path. There may be a sudden dawning of certainty about a relationship, deep understanding about the work you need to do, or a major shift in your thinking that brings peace and healing. All these experiences are moments of spontaneous awakening.

Not all moments of awakening are so dramatic. Often there may be small shifts and subtle changes in the way we see some aspect of life that slowly lead to a new awareness. Somewhere inside all of us there is a seed that seeks to grow towards the light. We may take a personal development class, join a yoga group or listen to audios from spiritual teachers who talk about the meaning of life and our unique place in the universe. This search may take many twists and turns, traversing rich, fulfilling experiences, as well as gleaning gems of wisdom from everyday challenges in relationships, work and family life.

This book is a gateway, an invitation to explore who you are, here and now, in this moment. It is a guide to your conditioned beliefs, illusions and expectations about many aspects of life. There are exercises, meditations and activities that you may incorporate into your day to help you live a more aware life, in each moment. All of this is simply a reminder of who you really are–your true essence.

By becoming more aware of your thoughts and emotions as they pass through you, and by tuning in to your own unique being, you are beginning to turn the key that will ultimately unlock a vast storehouse of treasures. All religious and spiritual traditions keep telling us in one form or another that the kingdom of heaven is within. You are your own saviour, your own divine work of art. You just need to become more aware of who you truly are. Only then can you reclaim your rightful inheritance of peace, love, freedom and joy, to fully live each sacred moment.

AWAKENING TO EACH MOMENT

This moment is your true reality. Here and now is where life can only be lived. The past is history; the future is mere conjecture. Life's truths are incredibly simple. Yet, due to conditioning that we have inherited from our families, our culture, and indeed from the whole human race, our thoughts reflect the uninvestigated beliefs that continue to cause pain, distortion, violence and deep confusion both within and without.

Focus in this moment on your breath. Feel your body naturally and without effort inhaling and exhaling the air that surrounds you. What are you feeling right now? Is there a feeling of discomfort or pain in any part of your body? What are you thinking right now? Just observe all that is passing through this body, mind and spirit that is your life. Now focus on your environment. Take a look

around you. Look at your surroundings. Are there any thoughts or feelings that come to the surface?

When you begin to do the exercises that are interspersed throughout this book you may begin to notice all the internal noise that you are living with. Listen to the noise of your thoughts with all those beliefs, opinions and comparisons. Listen, as an observer or witness, to this running commentary that passes judgement on everything and everyone you encounter. You may begin to ask: Where are these thoughts coming from? Are they new thoughts or are they old thoughts that have collected within me over years?

You may begin to wonder if you have learned or inherited these thoughts from your father, from your sister, from your best friend, from your partner or from some other significant person in your life. Maybe then you'll ask: Who is it that is doing the thinking? Perhaps later you may ponder: Who is it that is observing these thoughts?

We have been told that what separates human beings from animals is our consciousness, our ability to think and to reason. It is time that we challenged this most basic assumption that we are indeed conscious. Perhaps we need to ask: What am I conscious of? Am I only conscious of all that has gone before, of all the old thoughts that keep leading the human race to hatred, to fear, to destruction and to deep isolation?

We need to begin to feel the deep division within our own mind that separates us from every other living creature. How often do I fully experience the presence of a loved one, or the beauty of a natural setting, completely free from jabbering thoughts that force my attention away from the actual moment?

The following sections deal with various themes, such as creativity, joy, desire and love. Each section offers exercises that gently challenge our preconceived ideas, values and beliefs. Becoming truly conscious is a process of taking nothing for granted. It is a starting point where we observe, then question our every thought as to its level of truth and validity. Being alive in this moment means that we have our faculties finely-tuned, so that we can more readily respond to life's joys and challenges. Becoming conscious is a personal step on your path to inner transformation. Yet it is also a vital collective step towards a new global and social consciousness.

The process of becoming conscious needs a gentle hand to guide it. No amount of forcing yourself to gain awareness will bring the slightest benefit. We cannot demand change. We can only open to the process of moment to moment awareness, accepting ourselves as we actually are in the now. It is part of developing consciousness to notice how our thoughts may demand change and perfection in a preconceived way. Your only part in all of this is to observe, to be aware of your thoughts and feelings, and to allow them to pass. Above all, you need to develop patience, to allow your inner wisdom to guide you towards growth and transformation in your own unique time.

Teasing out a Practical Example

Below is an example of a real-life situation to illustrate how our thoughts have such a profound influence on our lives, moment to moment.

The Trigger

Marie awakens on a sunny Sunday morning. Already she has many plans and expectations for the day. Her partner still lies sleeping beside her. Yesterday they talked about beginning to work on the garden, cleaning away a real eye sore and preparing it for growing herbs and wild flowers. Marie is bursting with enthusiasm. In her mind's eye, she sees them rising early, showering together as they often do, having a lovely breakfast, bringing the dogs for a walk and then getting stuck into the gardening for a couple of hours, before meeting their friends for a planned lunch. Tom opens his eyes and smiles. Marie gives him a hug and tells him she's really looking forward to beginning their new project together. Tom groans and mutters he's too tried to think about gardening. "Let's work on it next weekend". He turns over and soon falls into a heavy sleep.

The Feelings

Marie is feeling frustrated, disappointed and annoyed. This is something they had planned together.

The Thoughts

Thoughts that run through Marie's head include Tom's selfishness and his inability to make plans. Memories are sparked of other times that they'd agreed on some task but then when it came to the day or the time Tom didn't feel like doing it. Marie usually gets completely taken over by these thoughts and feelings, believing that her day is ruined once

Tom backs out of a plan. She usually distances herself from him. Then she loses all loving feelings for him and instead focuses on blaming him for being selfish and uncaring. Marie tries to cut away all need for love and relationship but this only adds to her feelings of pain.

The Result

When Marie feels and thinks this way, she feels angry, extremely distant from Tom and continues to blame him and to snipe at him whenever she gets the chance. Tom usually apologies and tries to make it up to Marie but when Marie doesn't respond to his attempts, he begins to ignore her and to focus on things that he enjoys doing. This usually annoys Marie even more.

Truths

When we read the above scenario we may rightly ask: Who is right? Who is wrong? How can we have better relationships?

Shouldn't we stick to plans that we've made? Isn't it normal to become angry if we're let down when someone has promised us something? What could I do in a similar situation that would be best for all concerned?

If Marie's feelings are constantly disturbed by Tom's change of plans, it will be important for her to talk to him, to see if they can work out a better way to make and carry out plans that suit both of them. If Marie chooses to talk to Tom about her feelings, it is important that she first gives herself time and space to allow her feelings of frustration to recede.

It is important to note that we cannot force anyone to think or to feel as we do and we need to be open to hear their truth or to know when someone is having difficulty carrying out a task, such as in the case of a person who constantly procrastinates, promises everything but follows through on very little. Even in this case it is better to realise the truth than to keep on blindly making plans and feeling frustrated when plans are not carried out.

Using a Journal

You may wish to keep a journal to record any insights or comments that occur as you work through the various exercises that follow. Writing down your responses to the exercises makes the whole experience more concrete and aids in the process of developing conscious awareness.

Working through the Exercises

You may work through all the sections in sequence as they occur in the book or you may prefer to work on specific topics that appeal to you. Perhaps you'd enjoy just opening the book at random and working on whatever section presents itself. You may also like to repeat certain exercises periodically. This may help you to gain insights into areas where you feel stuck or confused. But whatever way you wish to approach this book, be in the moment, with an open, non-judgemental attitude of love, compassion and kindness for yourself and others. Enjoy the unfolding of your own unique journey.

Doing the Meditations and Visualisations

You may wish to record yourself on your phone reading each meditation or visualisation and then to play it back. You may prefer to read through an exercise and then to recall the basic instructions while practising it. If you are doing the work with a partner you may take turns reading and doing the exercises.

Working in a Group

The book also lends itself to a group of people working together, perhaps taking it in turns to be the group facilitator or appointing one person to fulfil this role. Allowing each person time to reflect, to share their insights and to enjoy quiet time and silence too if that is their choice, will aid in creating a peaceful space for working through the various exercises that are of interest to the group.

THE CONSTRUCTED SELF

Who am I? Who is this person with a name and a past, loved ones, talents and hobbies, future dreams and a present life situation? This is the self, a construction based on our cultural influences, relationships, thoughts, emotions and experiences. This self is motivated by survival, by acquisition, by remembering both the pain and pleasure of the past, by fantasising and dreaming up a more glorious future.

The self believes that things and people must be constantly accumulated to ensure its survival. Hence, there is always a gnawing search to be more of something: more beautiful, more talented or wealthy, more loved, more qualified, more admired. This all-consuming need to enhance the self is the basis of much of our fear and pain. We cannot leave ourselves alone. Although we may sometimes feel in control of our lives, the fact is that we cannot stop thinking and we are often at the mercy of our thoughts and emotions.

Over a lifetime, the self may change superficially many times in many ways. Ten years ago I loved rock music but today I may prefer classical. This makes little difference to the true core of a person. Often we form an identity around things that we like and things that we are good at. There may be the mistaken belief that we need to keep on adding more to who we are: new interests, new skills and new objects. If we are trying to feel secure by filling our lives with more things, then, no matter how many things we acquire, the circle of desire and fear remains unabated.

Take a look at your constructed self. What is this self made up of? What labels do you attach to yourself? Do you often use a list of attributes to describe yourself, such as physical characteristics (beautiful, plain), personality (intelligent, dull), roles (teacher, unemployed), relationships (mother, girlfriend), possessions (house-owner, car-owner), self-judgements (successful, failure)?

Go through your list of self-attributes. Do any of these labels actually describe the essence of who you are?

How has this self changed over the years?

What instigated these changes?

What does this self most desire?

What does this self most fear?

Is there a core you that has never changed? Is there an essence beneath all of the labels and attributes that is actually directing your life? Perhaps you have felt this essence emerging in some rare moment. If so, try to describe it?

THOUGHTS AND EMOTIONS

Joan walks into a roomful of strangers. She feels uneasy and anxious. She can't spot her friend anywhere. If Joan observes her thoughts she will hear the following: 'All of the women here look better than me'; 'I don't fit in here'; 'I won't know what to say if someone talks to me'; 'I'll leave after five minutes if Linda isn't here'. Joan pours herself a drink and sits at the back of the room, browsing through her phone to pretend to be busy.

Alisha has been invited to the same party. She hardly knows anyone, yet she feels excited and happy to have been invited. Her thoughts are registering the following: 'This black dress really suits me'; 'It'll be great to make some new friends'; 'I really like the feel of this place'. Alisha goes up to the drinks table and waits until someone offers her a drink. She chats for a few minutes with Ken, the bartender for the evening. Ken then introduces Alisha to his friends, Cathy and Therese. The three girls get on like a house on fire.

Thoughts and emotions are the very foundation of the self. It may seem to you that your thoughts are original, that they are *your* own thoughts. By beginning to observe your thoughts and emotions you will be struck by the patterns that quickly emerge. When we are primarily unconscious and just drift through life without any awareness of our internal life, of where our thoughts and emotions originate from, we have little chance to gain clarity or understanding about our life situation.

Our thoughts and emotions are basically energy forms that are being dredged up from the subconscious, from the past. They are old reactions to experiences or ideas that have been passed onto us by someone else. Ethnological studies are fascinating as they show us that different cultures emphasise the expression of different emotions. For example, in one tribe laughter may be frowned upon and that emotion is rarely displayed, whereas in another tribe laughter is encouraged and so becomes abundantly expressed.

By becoming more aware of your thoughts and emotions you are actually giving yourself more choice as to whether or not these thoughts are relevant to this current moment. It may be helpful to ask yourself: Does this thought or emotion have any relevance to my life here and now? Is the content of this thought actually true?

Observe each thought, each emotion without judgement, without labelling it as good or bad. Just become conscious of the fact that thoughts and emotions come and go, most often without your conscious direction. In this way, you begin to glimpse many of the building blocks that make up the constructed self. This is the basis of being mindful, where you begin to observe what is happening inside you.

Thoughts

In this moment, observe what you are thinking. Jot down your thoughts in your journal. Try keeping a record of your thoughts at different times of the day, such as when you get up in the morning, after you've had lunch, before dinner in the evening, when going for a walk or just before going to bed.

Begin to analyse each thought that causes you pain. Test the reality of what that thought is saying to you. Perhaps it is not true after all. Investigate this in a balanced and fair way. Inquire into this. Reconstruct this thought from many perspectives. Rewrite this thought to achieve its optimum relevance and truth.

If I think the thought, 'I'm not good enough because I messed up', I feel pain and confusion. So, let me challenge this thought. Is this true? Perhaps there is a greater truth–'I am learning and it's ok to make mistakes'. Maybe I need to apply this revised judgement to others. When I think the thought, 'She isn't good enough because she got that wrong', perhaps I need to introduce the more accurate thought that, 'She is learning. It's ok for her to make mistakes'.

In this way we begin to see that our thoughts create a version of reality. What I think, I see. What I think, I feel.

What I think about you becomes true and defines you in my world.

Have you noticed any patterns in your thoughts? (For example, being judgemental, comparing yourself to others, etc.)

Are there any thoughts that preoccupy you?

How many thoughts are generated from your past? (For example, values and beliefs from childhood, etc.)

How many thoughts pertain to your future? (For example, positive and negative self-beliefs, etc.)

Are there any thoughts that just belong to now, to this moment?

Challenging Negative Thoughts

The work of Byron Katie (2000) is both inspiring and practical in teaching us to challenge negative thoughts. She does this by using four questions to test the level of truth of each negative thought that causes pain and then finally turning the negative thought around so that other thoughts are explored for their level of truth. According to Katie, the importance of challenging old negative thoughts that are holding us back and causing pain is vital to bringing light and insight into the darkest corners of our unawareness.

The four questions that Katie asks are:

- Is it true?

- Can you absolutely know that it's true?

- How do you react when you think that thought?

- Who would you be without the thought?

This involves opening to a new perspective and allowing the possibility that our thoughts may be biased and inaccurate.

The following exercise challenges these negative thoughts as they arise. It is best to work through this exercise using your journal so that discoveries may remain concrete.

When you have a thought that is causing you pain, you can question the absolute level of truth of this thought. Write down all the emotions and judgements that emerge around this thought, as far as possible. Write down all of your feelings, your pain, anger and frustration about the person, event or situation that is triggering the thoughts. Now check the validity of your thoughts and judgements. Are these thoughts absolutely true? Are there other thoughts that could be truer and more relevant for your life, here and now? Rewrite any new thoughts that emerge that could be equally true or more accurate. Now, see how that thought feels.

It is important to realise that we cannot force our thoughts to change. However, when we see with absolute clarity that a previously uninvestigated thought is false, then that thought will dissolve and no longer cause us pain. Try this out for yourself and note down the results in your journal.

Emotions

In this moment, observe what you are feeling. Jot down your emotions in your journal. Keep a record of your emotions at different times of the day. You may observe both your thoughts and emotions at the same time.

Are there any emotions that you feel very frequently?

Which emotions are generated from your past?

Which emotions occur around some future event?

Which emotions belong solely to this moment?

Is there anything occurring in this moment in your environment that is causing you pain, anger or unease? If you are feeling any negative emotion, does this feeling stem from a past situation or from an imagined future event? Is there any reason for you to feel pain now?

Observe your thoughts and feelings as they arise and fade in each moment. Is there a link between what you think and what you feel at any time?

Becoming Free from Blocked Emotions

When we were children emotions just flowed freely through us. Somewhere along the line we learned what to feel and what not to feel, how to react and which emotions to block. When particular emotions have become blocked or buried we may periodically be taken over by the force of that emotion. We may become pure anger, pure pain, pure hatred or pure jealously. Eckhart Tolle (1999) calls this accumulation of unexpressed negative emotion the pain body. Tolle states that we may become possessed by negative emotions that take us over like an alien entity. People may be tortured by past experiences and may be blind to the calm, peaceful presence that is there for them now if they could only experience it.

Brandon Bays (1999) writes that blocked emotions are the basis for most physical diseases and illnesses. Bays developed a process called 'the Journey' which helps people to move through layers of repressed or unexpressed emotions that have accumulated over decades. According to Bays, after dropping through all the emotional layers, what is left is the source of consciousness, pure feeling, universal connection and love.

Are there emotions that periodically overwhelm you so that you lose the person you really are? If so, try to

describe these emotions. What has triggered each one? How do you behave when you feel each emotion?

The next time you experience a surge of deep emotion, become conscious of exactly what you are feeling. Observe your thoughts. It is vital not to get caught up in those thoughts that have been fuelling your emotions for years. You may quickly become taken over by this body of repressed emotion when old negative thoughts merge with blocked emotions, so that they begin to feed each other. Take a deep breath and allow the blocked emotions to flow through you and dissolve. Feel the energy of these emotions being set free. Remain conscious in the moment during this process, observing all the thoughts and emotions that are emerging. It is imperative not to identify with either the thoughts or the emotions. These belong to the past but are emerging in this moment, to be cleared and healed.

Record any insights in your journal that emerge.

THE CONSCIOUS OBSERVER

As you read these words, take a few moments to observe your inner world here and now.

What are you thinking?

What are you feeling?

Our ability to reflect on our thoughts sets us apart from any other species on earth. How we manage this skill is important for our wellbeing and our existence. Now, consider this part of you that is doing the observing, that is watching your thoughts and emotions as they pass through your body and mind, the part of you that is conscious in this moment. Eastern mystics refer to this conscious state as the observer. This is the source of consciousness, the eternal living being that is your true essence and has no beginning or end. This conscious presence animates your whole life. It is a perfect intelligence that

37

regulates the functioning of your physical body and connects you to all other life forms and to the source of all life. Some people may call this pure consciousness 'God', others refer to it as 'Life force', 'the All that is', or 'Manifest being'. Whatever name or label we place on it is immaterial. Becoming aware of this energy, of this consciousness that permeates your whole being is the beginning of freedom from the limitations imposed by the fearful, clinging, unaware self.

Thought and Separation

In the moments and days ahead become more conscious of where you are, what you are thinking and what you are doing. You will most likely observe that thought is incessant. You glance through your window at a sunset. Perhaps for a moment you are awed by the beauty of the scene that unfolds before you. But in the next moment thought appears with its judgements and comments: 'Isn't it beautiful! The sky is full of colour!' Observe the moment in which separation occurs between actually experiencing the moment and merely processing or thinking about it. When you are no longer one with the sunset, when thoughts step in to label and categorise the event, then division has occurred.

It is our thoughts that create deep separation within our own being. It is our thoughts that create division between the self and all other beings. We have become completely identified with our mind and body, with the physical world of form. We may not feel any connection with the eternal being that is our essence. Therefore, fully connecting with another person or with nature is a rare event. Our thoughts keep us at a distance, propagating the false belief that we are separate and different. According to Krishnamurti (1991) thought has its place in the intellectual, mechanical and practical realms of life, but thought is completely misplaced in the area of relationship where it causes deep division and confusion.

So, what can you do about thoughts that appear uninvited and that bring about separation in the moment? Simply observe the process, the scene, the thoughts and your reaction to those thoughts. The following visualisation may help you to connect with the essence of your being that is beyond thought and emotion.

Visualisation Exercise to Connect with Your Inner Being

Become aware of your breathing. Calmly scan your body for any sensations that are present. Tune into any feelings that arise in your conscious awareness. Tune in to the energy that permeates your body and mind–your life energy. Feel the energy that is beyond your physical body. You may feel this as a tingling sensation in your hands and feet. If you are feeling deep emotion at this time it may take a while for the emotions to come to the surface and to be cleared. Keep focusing on your inner body, on your inner being.

When your emotions begin to be released you may feel a deep stillness, a deep sense of aliveness and peace. This is the source of all life, the eternal energy that connects you to all other beings. The more you can focus on this energy that permeates the physical realm, the easier it will be to feel it.

During each day, begin to tune into this energy and become aware of the reality of this moment, no matter where you are or what you are doing. Your attention will drift but this is fine. When this happens you can just bring your awareness gently back to the present moment. In this way you are reconnecting with your true essence and opening to the source of consciousness within. When you are ready, you can gently bring your awareness back to the reality of your physical body. Notice any changes in consciousness that occur.

BEAUTY

The natural universe is full of beauty, symmetry, luminosity and mystery. When you open to your own light and consciousness, it becomes difficult to walk through this world without constantly being aware of beauty. When thoughts assume their rightful place within the technical, the mechanical and the practical spheres of life, the spirit of consciousness is set free to revel in the magnificence of this earth existence. Thus beauty is revealed: in sunbeams pouring through a window, in a smiling face, in a purring cat, in a yellow daffodil, in all the glories that this physical realm has to offer.

When beauty is no longer defined by the confines of the limited mind, we see beauty in simple things, in tiny flowers that grow half-hidden in hedgerows, in minute gestures that envelop us in intimacy and love. A mind that is disconnected from essence cannot create or know beauty. Wonderful works of art, such as magnificent buildings, timeless paintings, inspirational books and transcendent music can only be created from the depths of one's source. We begin to realise that beauty and depth are inseparable. For example, there is physical beauty that is bound to fade and there is inner beauty that may develop and flourish when compassion and kindness have been shown to others, bringing a new depth and wisdom. Beauty may then reflect an inner radiance, a sublime stillness that calls us forth to connect and merge in natural awe and simple recognition.

All this beauty is uncovered when the light of your essence begins to permeate your body and to illuminate your mind. When spirit merges with flesh and your senses awaken, beauty comes pouring forth in sparkling colours, in symphonic sounds and glorious harmonies. Consciousness imbues your whole life with awareness of beauty–your work, your leisure, your surroundings and your relationships. Each is infused with a new integrity, a reverence, a divinity. We are inspired to act, to create and to live in new ways. When we have opened–heart and soul–to the wonders that surround us it is only then that we may recognise our own profound beauty.

Recall a time when you were moved by a deep sense of beauty. Describe this moment or feeling.
Wherever you are at this moment, take a look at your surroundings. Is there anything or anyone here that brings you a sense of beauty? If not, maybe you need to dig deeper to discover something that positively strikes you or perhaps you need to spend time in a place of natural beauty.

As you go about your daily life, become aware of all the beauty that infuses your world, both without and within.

SELF-EXPRESSION

When we begin to observe our thoughts and emotions, to let them pass through us but not to identify with them, a new awareness begins to dawn. In our usual unaware state we cannot stop thinking. Thoughts and emotions keep on surfacing, occupying most of our attention and pulling us away from awareness of the here and now.

When we begin to become aware, we can choose to think of a solution to a problem, or to plan towards a future goal. The quality of these thoughts is finer and clearer than your usual way of thinking. Conscious thought is not confined to the past. Conscious thinking springs from your essence and hence opens the door to your creativity, inventiveness and intuition. This is the source of your being, your link with the eternal.

You may wish to jot down your responses to the following questions in your journal.

List all the creative things you enjoy doing. This can include any activity such as decorating, dancing, drawing, gardening, hairdressing, cooking, writing, or taking photos, etc.

How do you feel when you are in the act of creating?

Being in the Flow

It sometimes happens that when we are involved in some creative endeavour, such as planting flowers, painting a room, or writing a poem, we step out of ordinary time and our thinking takes on a different quality, where there is no division. It is as though the dancer and the dance–our whole being and the activity we are involved in–have become one. This phenomenon has been referred to as being in the flow (Csíkszentmihályi, 1990) or having a peak experience. It is as though a portal has been opened during the process of creating. Our thoughts become less dense and move into the

46

realm of intuitive knowing, flowing from a place of greater clarity, vision and wisdom.

The next time you become engrossed in an activity and feel yourself 'in the flow', become aware of the quality of your thinking. How does it feel? Is this different from your usual way of thinking?

Visualisation for Seeking a Solution to a Problem or Planning for a Future Event

If there is a problem that you wish to seek a solution to, or a future event that you wish to make plans for, write it down in your journal. Now, sit in a comfortable chair and close your eyes. Take a few deep breaths. Observe any thoughts or feelings that arise. Allow the thoughts and feelings to pass through you without judgement. Become aware of your breathing. Begin to feel the energy field that permeates your physical body. Feel this source of life within you, in your hands and in your feet, at the base of your spine, in your stomach, in your throat, in your forehead and at the top of your head.

Now, consciously think of the problem that you seek a solution to, or the future event that you wish to develop a plan for. Be aware of any thoughts or feelings that arise. Take note of any symbols or sensations that surface. Just let the solution or the plan unfold in its own way. Stay with this process for five to ten minutes. When you have spent sufficient time, begin to focus on your physical body. Feel your body sitting in the chair. Slowly open your eyes. Take a big stretch.

Now immediately, record in your journal any thoughts, feelings or insights that surfaced during this exercise.

JOY

Joy is our true state. Yet, influenced by factors of culture, religion, early life experiences and disappointments, many become practiced in the active suppression of joy in their lives. When our thoughts are quiet and our emotions are settled, then joy may shine through and enhance whatever it is we are engaged in. Whereas pleasure and happiness occur when we obtain something that we want, whether a situation, a thing or the company of a person we relish being with, joy does not depend on external circumstances or on acquisition. Joy simply arises when there is space within, when layers of emotion no longer dampen-down our essence.

Perhaps you have experienced a deep feeling of aliveness when you are out for a walk in the midst of nature or when you silently watch a sleeping child and your awareness is fully in the moment. It is rare in our present world to speak of joy. We listen each day to people speaking about their levels of stress, depression and anxiety. Preoccupation with the self, with thoughts of the past or the future block out the present moment and this keeps our deeper state of awareness submerged.

Recall a moment when you felt joy—a deep feeling of truly being alive that arose from within.

Become aware of moments when you feel deep joy, peace and contentment. Notice the peace and stillness that exist in such moments. Does the feeling of joy have a different quality to feelings of pleasure or happiness?

As you go about your daily tasks, begin to remind yourself that, no matter what is happening in your life, you are alive now, a unique, divine being. Allow the joy that is naturally within you to shine forth.

AWAKENING FROM ILLUSION

There is no person or thing outside of you that can ever give you lasting happiness or security. Physical life is subject to the dictates of time where separation, illness, accidents, death and decay are constant reminders of our mortal temporal existence. Change is an ever-present reality of the human condition. This is one of the most difficult truths for us to face.

Living with the illusion that any aspect of physical life can be controlled always leads to pain and disillusionment. It is only by accepting the ebb and flow of life, and allowing situations to unfold in their own way, that we can learn to live a fully conscious life. Accepting what is—the reality of this moment, whether or not it fits in with our desires and expectations—is our road to freedom. It is only in this moment that we may experience the true miracle and beauty of life. It is only by dropping our illusions that we may receive the gifts of wisdom, compassion and understanding that the lessons of this physical world can bestow upon us.

When change occurs to shatter our perceived stability we often resist by clinging to old ways, by pleading that the person or thing we have lost will be restored, by wishing to reverse the clock and by denying that any change has in fact occurred. Of course, all our pleading and denials cannot change what is. We often find that the greatest pain is caused by resistance, by the perpetuation of our illusions.

When we are deeply shocked and distressed by a sudden loss it takes us time to process the truth of what has occurred. We may only be able to let pieces of the loss and change that is happening around us filter into our consciousness. This may be nature's way of protecting us in times of shock and trauma, allowing the mind and the heart to slowly take in the enormity of an event that may have shattered our world.

Take a few moments to record any insights or observations to the following:

Is there any person, thing or situation that you are clinging to for your security or happiness?

Can you think of ways that you may bring security and happiness into your own life, without relying on any person, thing or situation?

Whenever a situation occurs in your life—whether trivial or momentous—that you are resisting, observe your thoughts. Inquire as to the true source of your pain or anger as follows:

What expectations and desires led you to believe that this situation would be different than it actually is? Examine the illusions that you believed to be true.

Observe your emotions. How difficult is it to let go of your belief that this moment should be different than it actually is?

Be gentle with yourself. Realise that changes have occurred that may have rattled your world. Even at this level of awareness, it is still important to allow yourself time to adjust to new situations and to grieve for lost loved ones. The heart and soul may have carved out unfathomable depths and it is only natural to find it difficult to accept the loss of a loved one or the end of a situation, where you once felt safe and comfortable.

It may be impossible to view your life as a wonderful adventure when you are grieving. It is a time when you need a lot of support to help you get back on your feet. Allow yourself time to rest and to heal. Then in time, when you are ready to embark on another leg of your journey, you may begin to see the truth that the source of your joy, love and stability resides within.

LOVE

Human beings experience love in direct proportion to their level of consciousness. True love is our natural state. True love imposes nothing on another and in turn requires nothing but merely delights in the uniqueness of each being. Freedom is always an essential ingredient of true love.

Since pure, conscious awareness is as yet a rare state for human beings, the love that we feel at our present level of consciousness is coloured by several factors, including our conditioning, our desires and the behaviour of our beloved. We fall in and out of love. We create social formulas and rules within the parameters of which we are allowed to experience romantic and sexual 'love'. There may be moments of stillness when we feel a surge of pure love for another being. Sooner or later, however, most people become disillusioned with romantic love when they realise that happiness and security cannot be guaranteed by another.

We blame our partners for not accepting us, for not loving us, for not giving us what we need. The constructed self identifies completely with the beloved and may even seek to control and possess the object of affection. Confusion, anger, conflict, violence, pain and deep unhappiness most often result from unrequited love or failing relationships.

The focus of our love must be inward, in terms of connecting with the deep source of love that is our essence, and outward, in terms of loving others. It is a futile exercise to become caught-up in whether or not another person loves you. We can never control what another person feels for us. Indeed, we can never fully know what anyone else feels because that depends on their capacity to open to consciousness and hence their ability to experience true love.

A greater degree of clarity will ensue when we realise that our attempt to love others is part of our spiritual development. Love is not only about fun and romance: Love is the expression of our soul. When we begin to experience consciousness in the moment–outside of time, past or future–we may gain an awareness of what true love really is.

Beyond all the thoughts, emotions and conditioning, your essence is pure love. No one can ever take this away from you. This is the natural state of all beings. Love is an expression of our oneness with the whole of life. Love freely given is the ultimate gift to another person. While everything in the physical plane is impermanent, true love cannot end because it is at the very heart of our essence.

You may like to note down your answers to the following:

Whether you are in an intimate relationship or not, list the attributes you most desire in a mate.

Take each of the above attributes in turn. Why do you consider this attribute to be important?

If your mate, or potential mate, lost these attributes would this bring about a change in your feelings of love?

Again, take each of the above attributes in turn. Now apply them to yourself. Is this a quality that you have already developed in yourself? If not, consider how you might develop this trait in yourself.

Love and Acceptance

Observe any conditions you erect around love. This may help you to gain greater awareness as to what true love actually is. True love is complete acceptance of the other person. This does not mean that we must accept negative or destructive behaviour. It simply means that we can see past the conditioned responses and lack of awareness that are temporarily obscuring this person's true nature. There may be times when we need to leave a relationship that is interfering with our ability to grow or is causing us too much pain. True

58

love may then mean letting go, where we wish the person well and send them love and light.

The basis of true love is acceptance. In accepting and loving another, not as we imagine them to be but as they actually are, we are flowing with the reality of life and moving away from illusions that delude us and cause us confusion and suffering. There is nothing as clear as true love. Thus, we may only begin to love ourselves as we are, without demanding that we change some undesirable aspect or achieve some goal that is a requirement of the ego. True love emanates from within. By loving what is–all of yourself, just as you are in this moment–you may offer the same precious gift to another.

True love recognises the unity and oneness of all beings. This pure love requires a heightened state of sustained consciousness. When we feel true love for another it is not possible to experience its opposite–fear, hate, fury or jealousy. True love is not limited by the constraints of physical or mental attributes. True love knows its own magnificence at the deepest level of existence and therefore recognises the sacred beauty and inherent perfection of all other beings.

True love is so distant from our usual notions of loving that it may sound extraordinary that this kind of love could ever be experienced. Yet true love resides within and is naturally revealed when there is full awareness. When we finally experience true love–whether for a moment, a day or a lifetime–our whole life is full of love and we are no longer concerned about whether or not another person loves us. True love has no concern or agenda other than to simply love.

DESIRE

It is the Buddhist view that in order to end suffering we must first end all desire. This teaching stems from the fact that we will never have all our desires fulfilled. If we cling to this physical world of impermanence where all forms must eventually whither and decay, we will continually experience disappointment, sadness and pain. Of course, as long as we are in human form we will experience desire. Instead of battling against or denying our desires it is important that we bring them into conscious awareness.

Becoming aware of desire gives us a clearer understanding of our motivation and allows us to choose honest behaviours to achieve our dreams and to have our needs fulfilled. When we are aware, we can decide if the realisation of a desire is for the good of self and others. It is not selfish to feel desire or to have needs. All human beings experience desire. Selfishness occurs when we try to force another, by any means, including manipulation, to comply with our desires.

A practical example of this is where Martha has a desire to make a home and a life with John. It is important for Martha to be aware of this desire because it will help her clarify the steps needed to bring it to fruition. However, a desire that involves another person must take that person's desires equally into account. Therefore, if John does not want to set up home with Martha, she must let this precise desire go. She may, however, create a new goal that does not depend on John, by focusing on the essence of her desire, such as to meet a loving man who will want to make a home with her. This desire can then be sent out in light to the universe, knowing that when the time is right, and it is for the greater good, that her desire will be answered.

Desire Visualisation

Find a comfortable position in your chair. Close your eyes. Take a few deep breaths. Feel yourself beginning to relax. Now, allow yourself to visualise your greatest desires coming true. What do you most desire at this moment? What kind of career do you desire? What kind of relationship would you like to have? What kind of future do you most desire? Notice the thoughts and feelings that accompany your desires. Spend about ten minutes on this exercise. Then, in your own time, open your eyes and take a big stretch.

Now, take a few moments to jot down answers to the following:

What is it I most desire in this moment?

What is it I most desire in my career?

What do I desire in my relationships?

What do I desire in my leisure pursuits?

What is it I most desire for my future?

Now, take a few moments to look at your answers. In each case, what is the essence of your desire? Are you searching for success, love, freedom, security, companionship, self-fulfilment, admiration, wealth, achievement, wisdom or some other underlying desire?

We invest so much time in career, relationships and leisure pursuits that we need to become more aware of the actual benefits we derive from each situation or experience. We need to become clear as to the particular need we wish to fulfil in our lives. We may need to reflect if a core desire is limiting our true development. The greater the clarity we develop around our desires, the more likely it is that we will remain at peace, whether or not specific desires are actually realised.

Look again at your answers to the above questions. Are there several desires that in essence reveal a similar need? For example, do you have a strong need to find love and companionship, and to feel secure? Or is your strongest

need a freedom one, wishing to travel and have many experiences out in the world?

Theories of Human Needs

Abraham Maslow (1943) and Dr. William Glasser (1985) developed theories as to the important role that our basic needs play in motivating our behaviour. Maslow developed the 'Hierarchy of Needs' pyramid, where our physical needs, such as for food and shelter, must be met before other needs become important, such as safety, belonging/love, self-esteem and self-actualisation. Glasser stated that we all have basic psychological needs that need to be met in order for us to feel fulfilled: Belonging, power, freedom and fun. He later added a sense of meaning to this core list.

Holding Our Desires Lightly

As human beings, very few of us have reached a high level of consciousness. Specific desires that we formulate in our minds

65

may not always be what we need most. Try to hold your desires lightly, emphasising the essence of the desire (such as one or more of Glasser's basic psychological needs, for example, belonging or freedom) more than any specific desire that you want to bring about. The visualisation on non-attachment in the next section may be used for this purpose.

NON-ATTACHMENT

Becoming attached to people, things and situations is part of the experience of almost every human being. Attachment develops when we identify with a person or thing and begin to believe that we need this for our happiness. But attachment is not love. In its most extreme manifestation, the self will do almost anything to keep the object of its attachment within its sphere of influence and control. An addiction to any person or thing leads to behaviours, such as manipulation, abuse and even violence. In its milder form, attachment is manifested as clinging, believing that the self is enhanced by the object of desire. Grief, rage or depression most often follows if loss of the object or person occurs.

As infants, we are deeply attached to our caregivers. We need these special adults to care for all our needs, for our very survival and growth. It is a major part of our emotional and psychological development to wean ourselves away from being attached to those we care for, towards loving in a positive and mature way.

Attachment is so ingrained in our culture that we take it as a normal way to relate. It permeates our songs, the films we watch and the ideals of dependent coupledom that many are encouraged to emulate. Loving another and sharing with another, appreciating an object or enjoying a situation: all may be deeply and fully experienced. The difference, however, between love and attachment is in the core element of freedom. Love never restricts the freewill of another nor clings to any person. Being attached holds the mistaken belief that the beloved in some way enhances the self. Fear and lack are driving forces behind attachment.

Being non-attached does not mean that you do not relate deeply to other people or that you do not enjoy life. Being non-attached may mean that you have faced the ultimate illusion, that anything in physical form can give you constant happiness. Then you can enjoy the riches and beauty of life without clinging to anything or any person, free from the need for a false sense of security or identity. Thus, there is an awakening from illusion. There is a realisation that we are separate in physical form, with our own freewill, and that change and impermanence are the very basis of physical life. Yet, by living in the moment, we are opening to a new consciousness where we may feel a connective energy or spiritual connection to all other beings.

In contrast to attachment, true love springs from the divine source within. Nothing can ever be added or taken away from an aware being. Love does not seek to possess or to capture. Love can only display its deepest nature by freely flowing and connecting in light with all other beings.

Moving from Attachment to Love

We may move from attachment to love in our relationships when we gain insight and understanding as to the reasons we cling to a particular person or situation. With insight and understanding comes awareness into our thought patterns, emotions, motivations and behaviours. Only then can we choose to let go of mistaken beliefs and ways of living that we once accepted as being natural and desirable.

By working through the following questions, you may gain some insight and understanding as to how and why attachments form. Open to the stillness that is deep within to inquire into these questions.

Is there someone or some situation that you are clinging to and deeply attached to?

What is it you need from this person or situation?

What would you do and feel if this person wanted to leave you or if a particular situation you are attached to ended?

Could you truly let this person or situation completely go? In the case of a person, could you still feel love for the person who has left you?

Now take a moment to look deeply inside yourself. How can you begin to bring love and joy into your own life? What can you do to treat yourself as you would a beloved? Make a list of any activities that come to mind.

Connecting with Source

No person, thing or situation is the source of your happiness. Nothing outside of you can ever fill the emptiness and aloneness that we all sometimes feel. There is something deep within that you need to connect with, to rely upon and to gain wisdom and inspiration from. This is the divine source that is your true nature. There is little to be gained in seeking love or approval from others. Being loved by another is a gift that we

71

have nothing to do with. We cannot create or control another's love.

Delighting in time spent and moments shared with people we love, enjoying things we appreciate in life, feeling content and fulfilled in particular situations such as fulfilling work, are all beautiful experiences. But we need to realise that we are all free spirits, passing through this world, seeking to overcome the limitations of our conditioning and to develop our capacity to love. Learning to love in freedom and practising non-attachment in this passing physical world are giant steps we may take towards growth in awareness.

ACCEPTANCE

In any situation we have three choices. Firstly, we may act quickly to solve a problem or resolve a situation. Secondly, we may find ourselves in a situation where we cannot act or we choose not to act, but where we may plan to bring about change in the future. Thirdly, we may not be able to change anything about our situation and so we may choose acceptance in the present moment.

Acceptance means that we surrender to the reality of this moment. We can only surrender if we let go of all attachments to a particular outcome. Far from being a state of passivity, this is a very powerful state where we may regain our sense of freedom and awareness. An extreme example is where a person is imprisoned and hence loses physical freedom. When everything has been done to plead for release but this has failed, the best option is often to surrender, to accept the reality of the present situation. A person may not be happy being imprisoned, but may feel a sense of inner freedom in choosing to surrender to the moment and making the best of the situation.

Is there any situation in your life that is causing you great stress? If so, what steps have you taken to find a solution? Are there any other steps you may take towards finding a resolution?

When you have done your utmost to change a situation or when the solution is not within your control, then it is time to surrender to the reality of the moment. Become aware of any resistance there is to surrendering, to giving up the struggle to find a solution. Also, become aware of how it feels to stop struggling and to surrender, to be patient and to allow the situation to resolve itself in its own way.

The following visualisation may be used to formulate your desire while also surrendering to whatever outcome occurs.

Acceptance Visualisation

Write down your desire or the problem that you seek a solution to on a piece of paper. Now, sit comfortably and close your eyes. Visualise yourself standing on a hill overlooking a vast expanse of sky. Perhaps it is night-time and you are gazing up at the stars, the moon and the planets in all their magnificence. Perhaps it is daytime and you are watching the clouds float across a turquoise sky. Now, ask the universe to grant your desire for the good of all and when the time is right. See yourself holding up the paper where you have written your desire. Now, gently let the paper float away into the vastness of space. As you watch the sheet float up into the sky consciously choose to let go of any attachment you have to your desire being fulfilled. Trust that your desire will become manifest if this is the best solution for all concerned.

Take a few moments to sit and relax in the stillness. Then take a deep breath, stretch and open your eyes.

Surrender and Acceptance

Surrender occurs when there is full acceptance that we cannot control the outcome of a situation and so we open to the reality of the moment. This can be a great relief because we no longer have to search for a solution we are powerless to find. Observe any changes in your thoughts and feelings when you surrender to what is happening in the here and now. You may feel a greater sense of peace and calmness flowing through you as you accept and let go.

IMPERMANENCE

We know in our minds that all of life is impermanent. We see this in the changing seasons, in the many losses and 'little deaths' we all experience in our relationships, in work, and in the very fabric of life. However, at an ego level the self refuses to believe that there will ever be an end to physical life. We keep clinging to people, things and situations, believing that we will somewhere find a stability and security, free from pain and disillusionment.

The security we seek can never come from outside us. All the money in the world cannot give us complete security. It is at the level of awareness that we may suddenly realise one of nature's foremost laws: eternal life is the way of the spirit, but impermanence and mortality is the way of all physical life.

List all the people and things in your life that you feel love for.

Try to discover the essence of the gifts that each person or thing brings to your life.

Can you accept that all these people and things that are part of the physical world are merely passing through this life, as you are yourself? Observe your thoughts and emotions. Do you feel pain, anger, distress, acceptance or some other emotion when considering this?

Visualisation Exercise to Focus on Impermanence

Choose one person who you feel a lot of love for and who you would find it particularly difficult to let go of. It may be a loved one who you are already parted from through death or separation. Visualise this beloved person standing in front of you. Allow yourself to feel the flow of love between you. Realise that the true essence of the love you feel can never be lost. Impermanence is a feature of the earth plane. All is eventually lost in physical form, while the love you feel for a person is eternal.

Now, visualise this positive eternal love as a source of light that shines above both of you. See that each of you is connected to this light, and that ultimately the light connects the two of you from its brilliant source. This light is pure consciousness that connects you in love to all other beings. Allow yourself to feel this eternal light energy, this true love, flowing through every pore and channel of your being. Know that this love is your true self and can never die.

Take some time to rest in the stillness that surrounds you. Then when you are ready take a deep breath, stretch and open your eyes.

Take a few moments to jot down in your journal any feelings, thoughts or insights that arose for you during these exercises.

FREEDOM

Freedom comes from living your own life, focusing on your own issues and taking care of yourself–your body, your mind, your interests, your work and rest-time. Becoming lost in other people's lives or interfering with their way of life is a kind of slavery. Finding the truth of who you are is at the core of authenticity. Inquiring into old beliefs that arise and may need to be questioned as to their relevance and truth is the path to freedom.

Ultimate freedom is realising your oneness with all other beings and feeling your eternal connection to the source of all life. This realisation exposes the core illusion: that anything in the physical world is worth clinging to or grasping after. True freedom lies in this moment, in being conscious here and now and in allowing life to unfold in its own unique way.

You become free by making peace with whatever is happening in this moment, by learning to accept life as it is instead of the fiction of what should be, which has been concocted by your confused thoughts. Respect life as your teacher. Use your emotions to guide you to areas where further learning is needed. When you flow with life, without putting up resistance to the twists and turns in circumstances that come your way, you have reached the gateway to freedom.

You are free when you accept yourself, other people, situations and indeed the entire universe as it is. Of course, this does not mean that we allow ourselves to be abused in anyway. From a position of acceptance you can go out into the world, planning, creating, yet always facing the truth of what is. Then you are free to live, to love, to be still and to act, responding in awareness to the requirements of this moment.

Go through the following questions and record any comments or insights in your journal.

What is it that you need to free up in your life?

81

Do you require freedom from thoughts, emotions, self-judgement, relationships, work, home life, lack of money, lack of self-worth?

Freedom Visualisation

Sit back in a comfortable chair. Close your eyes. Take a few deep breaths and begin to move deeply within. Take a few moments to consider each of the following: Do you regularly give yourself the gift of love, of self-acceptance, of fun-time, of space and alone time? What does freedom look like to you? What would it be like to allow yourself to choose freedom?

Relax for a moment in the peace that envelopes you. Now slowly open your eyes. Record any insights in your journal.

Freedom and Love

It is only when we are internally free—when we have taken responsibility for our own lives, have chosen to pursue our authentic path and have accepted ourselves as we are—that we may truly love and open to another person. Being free does not mean that you can never be committed to a person or to the fulfilment of a goal. Often people say they need to be free when in fact they are slaves to fear and past traumas, not having developed the capacity to feel love or commit to another. Being conscious of your natural internal freedom means that you may freely choose the people and activities you wish to devote your time and energy to. Loving in freedom means that you consciously choose to be committed to another, while allowing your beloved the freedom to follow his or her own path.

When we awaken to consciousness, we become aware that we may never possess another person and that we may never be possessed. The flowering of love occurs when there is total acceptance of self and other and when both are always free to pursue separate lives yet choose to be together.

Jot down in your journal any insights or comments that occur for you around freedom.

PEACE

We strive for so many things in this life. We believe we will be happy when we obtain a desired person, situation or object. Happiness is so fleeting and cannot last as it is just an emotion that will change when life doesn't give us what we want or takes away what we most value. I have come to learn that deep down we are really seeking peace of mind. Although life changes will sometimes shake our state of peace, it is well worth the investment to find ways and means of bringing more peace into our lives.

Worry, anxiety, depression and sleeplessness are on the rise. This all boils down to our thoughts running wild, imaging all kinds of dire scenarios, blowing everything out of proportion, believing that times of joy and love will never again happen because of a loss or disappointment. Allowing these thoughts and accompanying emotions to surface is the first step to freedom. Then we need to bring in the gentle, guiding voice of reason, to bring our focus back to this moment and to know that all we can manage is what we are doing right now. We may set aside time later in the day or the following day, when we may feel more balanced and less overwhelmed and draw up a basic plan, to help us deal with the situation we find ourselves in.

Describe a place or a scene that fills you with peace.

Recall a special place where you have felt peaceful and safe. This may be a natural setting or a place where you remember feeling relaxed, such as a garden, a park, a café, a favourite room or a comfy chair in your home. Focus on the feelings and sensations around you that bring a peaceful feeling. This may be your special peaceful place that you might want to recall whenever you are feeling stressed, anxious or ill at ease. Allow the peace that this setting evokes to flow into your heart and your mind, restoring your feeling of balance and tranquillity.

Peace Meditation to Still Thoughts and Welcome Sleep

If it is night-time and you are finding it difficult to sleep, the following short meditation may help you to let go of all those thoughts that are cluttering your mind, give you the space you need for peace and to allow sleep to enter.

Begin by closing your eyes. Now imagine there is a beautiful light just under your feet. Slowly see this shimmering light beginning to flow up over your toes and feet, flowing over your ankles, moving up along your calves, easing out any strain or tiredness from your calf muscles. The light continues to flow over your knees and along your thighs, gently massaging and healing as it flows. It is now flowing upwards over your hips, lower back and abdomen, filling your back, chest, hands and arms with soothing and healing energy.

The light is now flowing up over shoulders and neck, easing out any tension. It is moving higher now, gently flowing over your mouth, cheek bones, eye-sockets and all over your face. Now feel the light spreading up over your forehead, bringing you a warm loving feeling as the light flows over your head. Now your entire body is full of light. You feel deeply relaxed, safe and at peace. Continue to relax and to breathe evenly and regularly.

In a few moments you may choose to clear your mind from any thoughts that are worrying you or keeping you from getting a good night's sleep. You can remind yourself that you can take all these thoughts back in the morning if you decide to do so. Tomorrow, you may choose to work on solutions to any problems you feel you need to resolve. But for now, there is nothing you can do to solve anything and it is in your best interest to clear your mind and to make space so that you can drift into a peaceful sleep.

Begin by visualising a large basket beside your bed. You may see a wicker basket, a laundry basket, a large container or a box. This is where you may place any worries or thoughts you have that are causing you anxiety. You may visualise a scene, a situation or a person that is the source of your worry, or you may hear words or feel sensations. Just allow them to come up, one by one and. When each one arises, just place it in the basket. Your basket may expand to any size so don't worry about it filling up. You may continue doing this until you feel there are no more thoughts or worries that you need to let go of.

Now, allow your mind to dwell on that special place where you feel safe and at peace. Smell the fragrances, see the colours, feel yourself in that scene, relaxing, unwinding, stretching, closing your eyes, feeling safe and at peace.

Allow the tranquillity of this scene and the restfulness of this moment to bring you into a peaceful sleep.

SPACE

There is so much spoken about the need for space. Most often this need is internal and there is a craving to be alone, to have time to reflect, to regain emotional balance or to experience inner clarity. Space may be a necessary elixir after many hours of supporting others or of responding to external demands. The need for space may also include the need for silence, to find a quiet place and to finally listen to your own internal dialogue.

At this moment do you need to grant yourself the gift of space? Is there a moment you can create today where you can feel free, unfettered and undisturbed?

One experience that springs to mind is awakening early just before dawn and going out into the garden. The earth feels full of sleep and all is still. Glancing upwards, it is difficult not to be awestruck by the black sky that shimmers with thousands of glittering stars. Inhaling the cool dark perfume of this slumbering garden adds to the intoxication of the moment. Now, there is an immense sense of space. Here, staring up at the vastness of the cosmos, it is easy to become part of this enormous mystery, this incredible beauty.

Where can you find one moment's feeling of spaciousness today?

Instinctively we turn to nature to remind us of our own spaciousness, of our inherent links with the depths of the oceans and the majesty of the cosmos. Our senses heighten and our souls rejoice when we come face to face with the natural beauty of a snow-capped peak, a stunning canyon or a sparkling sea.

Close your eyes. Feel your feet on the floor and bring yourself fully into this moment. Can you allow yourself to feel completely free now, with nothing to do except live simply in tandem with this universal spaciousness?

Tune into your emotions. Is there an emotion that needs to be acknowledged and set free? Just allow this emotion to be felt by you. Is there something you need to do or say that will help this emotion to move through you?

Tune into your thoughts? Is there some painful thought that keeps nagging and interfering with your natural state of peace? Is there something you need to do or say that will allow this thought to recede?

Sometimes, when we need space to look inwards, we feel too tired and simply make do with watching a movie or reading a book. We seek entertainment as a distraction to cover over the choppiness that we know resides in our inner world. The arts are marvellous forms of entertainment and provide endless ways of learning and reflecting. Maybe we just need to be aware sometimes if we are watching, listening or reading in an attempt to cover up what is really niggling us within.

In a busy, demanding world it is vital to know how to recharge your emotional and spiritual self. Sharing your life and space with loved ones and opening to the responsibilities of work and relationships, need to be balanced by reflective time, and by discovering the vast spaciousness within.

JUST THIS MOMENT

This moment is all there is. What can my actions do now to affect the events of yesterday? What of tomorrow–how certain am I that what I have planned to do next week will ever come to pass? Only this moment is certain as it unfolds in its own way. Only in this moment can my actions make a difference. When I am awake and aware that this moment is unique, then I have choice as to how I wish to act, now. When I slumber in old thoughts and emotions, I become lost and miss out on what is happening now in this living, breathing moment.

When you do the following exercises you may like to write down your experiences in your journal.

Bring yourself fully into this moment. Take a look around you. Wherever you are going to or coming from realise that this is where you are right now. Look inside yourself.

Are your thoughts and feelings part of this living moment, or are they residing elsewhere, in past or future?

How does it feel to be awake, to be alive in this moment?

No matter what you need to do tomorrow, or what you feel you should have done yesterday, ask yourself, is there anything you need to do right now?

When you are in the present moment your thoughts may drift to memories or future plans. Acknowledge these thoughts and feelings. Yet, realise that the thought that is dragging you away from this moment may be causing you pain, stress, or tension.

Ask yourself how life would be right now if you were not focused on a person or place that is not part of this moment. Would you feel less stress or tension?

Perhaps deep down there is an inner knowing that you may find greater peace or happiness somewhere else, either alone or with another person. By paying attention to your feelings over time you will develop a strong sense of the right place for you to be.

Experiencing Life in This Moment

When you are alert and aware you may feel a greater clarity as to the tasks you need to perform. Listen to the intelligence and wisdom within to guide your life and actions in every moment. Constant awareness in the moment is freedom from time—an eternal life of moment-to-moment alertness. Being present in this moment is the only place where you can ever experience life.

MEDITATIONS TO INCREASE

AWARENESS

Visualisation and meditation stem from an ancient tradition that advocates the inward journey to increase awareness and bring about deep peace and healing. The meditations here may be used as often as you like to help develop an awareness of the energy and stillness that is at the core of your being. The light meditation is particularly suited to being practiced in the early morning before rising and in the late evening before retiring. The connecting in love meditation may be practised as a reminder of your unity with the whole of life. The breath meditation allows you to connect with the powerhouse of your divine being. This will help you to become conscious of the cyclical nature of thoughts and emotions as they arise, occupy the mind and body, and then pass through you. By tuning in to the deeper levels of your being, you may become more attuned to experience the peace, joy and wisdom that is always present.

Preparation Before Meditation

For each of the following meditations set aside quiet time and space where you will not be disturbed. It is better not to meditate on a full stomach. Allow ten to twenty minutes for each exercise. Preferably, sit in a comfortable but supportive chair where your spine is straight. This is the best position for relaxing while remaining focused and not drifting into sleep.

You may wish to record yourself on your phone reading each meditation and then to play it back when doing the meditation. You may prefer to read through each meditation and then to recall the basic instructions while practising it. If you are doing the work with a partner or in a group you may take turns reading to each other and doing the meditations.

Recording your observations

After each meditation you may use your journal to record the following observations:

How did you feel during the meditation: relaxed, anxious, content, restless, peaceful, or did you experience other feelings?

Did any thoughts you consider to be important or relevant surface?

Did any emotions you consider to be important or relevant surface?

Did any part of your body feel particularly tense or painful?

Did you experience any deep feelings, such as stillness, love, beauty, joy or peace?

Did you receive any insights during or after the meditation?

In the early stages of meditation you may find it difficult to focus and to relax due to surfacing thoughts and emotions. Most of us are so used to packing our days full of tasks and people that we rarely give ourselves space, to simply be alone and connect inwards. Regular practice of meditation will bring deep peace and clarity as your consciousness begins to awaken.

LIGHT MEDITATION

Begin by closing your eyes. Now imagine there is a beautiful golden light just under your feet. You can feel this shimmering light begin to flow up over your toes, relaxing and soothing your feet. It is now flowing over your ankles, moving up along your calves, easing out any strain or tiredness from your calf muscles. The beautiful light is now spreading over your knees and is now moving higher along your thighs, gently massaging and healing as it flows. It is now flowing under your chair and beginning to move upwards over your hips and your lower back. Feel your back beginning to be filled with this soothing and healing energy.

The light is now flowing up through your spine and spreading out all over your back, to gently massage away tension from every muscle. The light is moving up over your shoulders, relaxing and energising, releasing all tension from your shoulders. Now the light is flowing down your arms. You can feel its gentle energy radiating over your elbows. It is now flowing down over your wrists and hands, spreading out to relax each of your fingers.

The light now moves over your abdomen and begins to flow upwards over your stomach. Glowing and shimmering, the light flows up over your chest. Now it is moving higher over your collarbone and up along your neck, again easing out any tension that might have accumulated with the stresses and strains of life. Now the light flows up over your face, moving over your mouth and nose, flowing over your jawbones, releasing all tension, soothing and healing. Feel these beautiful light rays penetrating to the very core of your being, bringing deep love and peace.

The light is now flowing up over eyes, healing and gently massaging your eye-sockets. Now, feel the light spreading up over your forehead, spreading its beautiful brilliant rays over your skull, bringing you a warm loving feeling as the light flows over your head. Now your entire body is full of light. You feel deeply relaxed, safe and at peace.

Focus on this light that is coursing through your veins. Feel the light bringing deep healing and balm to every muscle, every bone and every fibre of your being. Become fully aware that you are an eternal being of light. Focus on the feeling of oneness, of love and peace that emanates from the core of your being. Continue to feel this essence deep within. Your essence is connected to the source of all life. Spend a few minutes allowing the light to penetrate further into every crevice of your being, bringing deep healing and joy to every muscle and every cell.

Now in your own time become aware of your body sitting on the chair. Become aware of your hands resting on the chair or in your lap and your feet resting on the floor. Slowly open your eyes and come back into the room, feeling refreshed and full of light.

CONNECTING IN LOVE TO ALL BEINGS

Close your eyes. Take a deep breath and begin to feel yourself relaxing. Take another deep breath and feel yourself moving into a natural state of deep peace and stillness. Now, begin to feel the love that emanates from deep within. True love is your very essence. Become aware of this divine love that is your true nature, the life force that sustains you in every moment. Feel this love flowing into the depths of your being. This is the same love that permeates all of life and connects you to all other beings.

Perhaps you would like to visualise a guardian angel, a spirit guide, or a symbol of divine love standing by your side. Feel the light streaming from this source of love and guidance, showering you with pure love and healing.

Feel this love flowing through every cell of your being. Spend a few moments basking in the rich glow of love that emanates from you and that surrounds you.

Now visualise your love as a beautiful radiant light that connects you to all other beings and to all other life forms. Feel this love connecting with the loving essence of every being in the universe and spreading outwards throughout the entire cosmos. Enjoy this feeling of shared love and connection for a few more moments. This love is your true essence. You may feel this radiant love within when you open to the here and now, when you become conscious of being in the moment.

When you are ready, bring your awareness back to your body. Notice how your body feels, being supported by the chair. Now, in your own time, open your eyes and take a big stretch, just as a cat does after taking a nap and before beginning its day.

FOCUSING ON THE BREATH

Begin by closing your eyes. Focus on your life energy. Feel it flowing through your body. Now, pay attention to your breath as you inhale and exhale. The breath is the very basis of life. It is a gateway through which you may access your deepest self, the source of all life and the divine that connects you to all other life forms.

As you focus on your breathing, thoughts and feelings arise. Become aware of each thought and feeling. Observe without judgement as the thoughts come to the surface and then fade to be replaced by others. Likewise, observe without judgement any emotions that bubble into your awareness. Observe how various parts of your body feel. Is there any place in your body that feels tense or painful? If so, continue to breathe deeply. Visualise your breath flowing into that area of your body, clearing away any tension or pain.

Continue to focus on the breath for a further 10 to 15 minutes, while allowing any thoughts or feelings to surface and then to pass through your mind and body. Keep bringing your awareness back each time to your breath. Perhaps you are beginning to get a sense of this life giving energy–this inner spirit that is the powerhouse that keeps you alive and breathing, moment after moment. Feel the energy emanating throughout your physical body. Now, become aware of this energy flowing from your inner body. This is the core of consciousness, the source of your love, joy, beauty and peace. This is your true nature, your divine being. Feel this energy radiating from deep within, connected to the source of all life.

Now, slowly become aware of your hands resting on the sides of the chair or in your lap. Feel your feet planted firmly on the floor. Feel your body being supported by the chair. Slowly open your eyes and take that big cat-stretch again.

ACTIVITIES FOR WAKING-UP

There are many powerful activities that we may incorporate into our daily lives to stimulate awareness. The activities outlined in this section may help us to awaken to the simple reality of life as it unfolds in each moment. These everyday activities involve going for a walk, doing a piece of artwork and spending time in nature. These are but examples of many common activities that become imbued with consciousness when we fully focus on what we are doing in this moment.

WALKING WITH AWARENESS

One of the greatest gifts I ever gave to myself was the time to walk almost every day. I usually walk two to three miles, sometimes in the morning, most often after lunch, and in summertime in the long bright evenings. When I lived in Dublin, Ireland, I walked into the city each morning from Chapelizod. For the years I lived in Santa Clara, California, I varied my walk between two neighbourhoods, Ulistac on Lick Mill, and the area behind the Rivermark Mall. In Wexford Town, in Ireland, I'm spoiled for choice but I favour one route that leads to the Slaney and the north part of town.

Walking not only rejuvenates the body but it may become a marvellous practice in moment-to-moment consciousness. You may easily and gently become aware of the totality of the moment and of your inner world, while focusing on the outer physical universe of sight, sound and sensation. Watch your thoughts and emotions as they bubble up, catch hold of your attention and then slide away to be replaced by others. Become aware of your feet making contact with the pavement or grass, the wind blowing through your hair and on your face, the rise and fall of your breath and the rhythmic movement of your arms and legs. Feel the energy that coordinates all of your physical self that keeps on flowing, even when you lose conscious awareness of it. Observe the world around you that is moving and static, flowing and solid: the cars, other walkers, houses, trees and gardens, yapping dogs and playful children.

When I first started walking alone regularly I felt an incredible feeling of liberation. I quickly began to feel a connection with people and things as I glided by in a kind of cosmic dance. I also began to realise how often I get lost in daydreams, thinking and emoting about all kinds of situations and people. How I so often lose connection with my senses! How little I actually see or hear of the real world around me! The way forward, as in every one of these exercises, is to observe the workings of the mind and then, without judgement, to allow the thoughts and emotions to be, but also to become aware of being in this moment, whatever that reality entails.

So try it for yourself. Plan to take a walk at least once a week but over time you may increase this to several times a week. If you can make the time, try walking every day. You can walk for any length of time, though it may be wise for a person not used to exercise to begin walking for just a few minutes and then to slowly increase the length of your walk.. I like to walk at a quick pace, whereas others may prefer a slow ramble. Choose a day and time that suits. Simply choose a route where you can walk from your door, or choose some other location like a park or a nearby beach that is easily accessible. Be sure that you walk in a safe area where you feel relaxed, secure and you can really enjoy the experience. If you have a dog as a companion on these rambles then this may greatly add to the fun for both of you.

When you return from your walk spend a few moments noting down any insights in your journal. You may wish to jot down your responses to the following:

When I walk I am most aware of:

Thinking: Did I observe my thoughts in a non-judgemental way, regardless of their content?

Emoting: Did I allow any arising emotions to flow through without interference?

Breathing: Did I use my breath to return my thoughts to the present?

Taking in the people and scenes around me: Did I feel my connectedness to my environment in each moment?

Feeling various sensations in my body: Did I scan my body and send healing light to any areas of tension?

Being full of energy: Did I feel changes in my energy levels, when particular thoughts or emotions emerged?

Some other observations to consider:

Was there any pattern to thoughts or emotions during your walk that you became aware of?

During your walk did you suddenly become aware that you had been lost in thought?

How did you feel after your walk?

Did you gain any insights into life issues or concerns during your walk?

Walking with awareness is a great gift that you can give to yourself no matter what age you are, what limited resources you have or where you live. Walking is a wonderful experience that you can enjoy anywhere. Allow yourself to open to the world around you and to the consciousness that is your inheritance.

AWAKENING ARTWORK

A combination of artwork and visualisation may be used to gain healing and insight into life issues that are causing pain or confusion. Even people with no art experience whatsoever can tap into their natural creativity to do this exercise. Symbols are the language of the subconscious mind but also of the higher consciousness, the source of our inner wisdom and healing. By accessing symbols that represent our pain and our path to healing, we may develop a greater awareness and freedom from unresolved emotions and life situations. The visualisation and artwork below are based on the work of Barbara Ganim and Susan Fox (1999).

Materials Required

You will need a large sheet of blank white paper, wallpaper or a sheet from a sketch pad of about A2 size. You can use either crayons, felt tipped pens, coloured pencils or paints. Try to have at least ten colours of whichever medium you choose so you won't be restricted in your use of colour. Before you begin the visualisation, place your materials on the floor or on a table where you can have immediate access to them.

Intention: To examine a source of pain

Open your journal. Sit quietly for a few moments and contemplate a life issue that is causing you pain. Now, write out your reason or intention for doing this artwork. Describe the problem or issue you wish to receive clarity about. Now, choose a word or a sentence to describe this issue or problem. Write this title on the top of the blank sheet that you will be doing your artwork on.

Visualisation

Sit in a quiet, comfortable place. Close your eyes. Take a deep breath. Feel yourself relaxing more deeply with every breath that you take. Continue to breathe deeply for a few moments.

Visualise a golden healing light under your chair. Now, see this light spreading upwards, flowing up over your feet and legs, over your chest and arms, over your shoulders and your head.

Now allow the title of your artwork to come into your mind. Ask your higher consciousness to show you a symbol or picture that will help you to gain clarity around the situation that is causing you pain or confusion. Notice any colours, shapes or images that arise. Focus for a few moments on any symbols or pictures that you are being shown.

Now feel yourself once again sitting in your chair. Gently, and in your own time, open your eyes. Take a big stretch.

Artwork

Reach for your paper and art materials. The picture or symbols should still be fresh in your mind. Take as long as you need to sketch, colour or paint what you were shown during the visualisation.

Interpretation

When you have finished your drawing or painting put it in front of you on the table or floor. Now jot down the answers to the following questions in your journal:

What do you feel when you look at your drawing?

What do each of the objects you have drawn mean for you?

What do each of the colours in the drawing mean for you?

What does the drawing tell you about how you feel emotionally?

Is there anything in the drawing that disturbs you? If so, describe it.

Is there anything in the drawing that you particularly like? If so, describe it.

Is there anything in the drawing that brings you a feeling of healing, or that offers a solution to your problem?

Looking at the drawing in front of you now, is there anything you would like to add to your artwork? If so, what would you like to include? What difference would this make to the drawing? (If there is some change you wish to make to the drawing then you may do so).

This artwork exercise may be used whenever you desire a solution to a problem, or when you wish to find greater clarity around your emotions.

NATURE–ACCEPTANCE OF WHAT IS

If you have done any of the exercises in this book you will have noticed that thought is virtually always a noisy companion. Thought is incessant, continuously throwing up images and memories of people, scenes and events. Perhaps during one of the meditations you may have noticed a moment of quiet, when the mind was not preoccupied with thought. There is yet another master, a profound guide to stillness and acceptance that we have not yet mentioned. This teacher both surrounds and sustains us. This teacher is nature.

The next time you come face to face with a flower, whether placed in a vase on your table or growing in a wild forest, take a moment to look at the delicate beauty of this living being. Observe its stillness, its perfection, its absolute acceptance of what is. It has its ordained place in the vast scheme of life. It may be blown hither and thither by wind and rain yet its quiet dignity, its essence of stillness, remains unmoved.

Animals too have much to teach us. Observe the quiet serenity and dignity of a cat as she sits in the centre of a sunbeam, complete in her own simple joy. Watch the friendly openness of a dog as he affectionately paws and licks his human companion. Our animal friends remain present and alert in the moment, without any internal division or separation.

Whenever you next find yourself by the seashore, walking in a forest, sitting in a park or garden, or crossing a country field, become aware of the profound acceptance that permeates all of nature. In nature, there is no opposition to what is. Here the seasons change and life unfolds in harmony with the natural cycles of life, death and rebirth. Every blade of grass, every grain of sand radiates its tranquil existence and its sacred grandeur. Perhaps in the depths of nature we too may learn to accept our place among the stars, the flowers and the oceans.

When you are next in nature sit down for a moment, breathe in the pure air and listen to the myriad of sounds that surround you. You may wish to ponder the following:

Is there any facet of nature that does not belong here or is out of place?

How do you feel surrounded by nature?

Do you feel a part of this natural environment?

Does being in nature help you feel a greater sense of your own unique place in this universe?

If you live in a town or city then at least once a month give yourself the healing treat of spending a few hours in nature.

Allow the innate wisdom and peace that is at the heart of raw nature to inspire and renew your whole being. This is one of the most glorious ways to raise your consciousness to an ever-deepening level. Soak up the beauty and peace of the natural abundance that permeates the whole universe and share in its vastness and consciousness.

REFERENCES

Bays, B. (1999), *The Journey*, Harper Element, London.

Csikszentmihalyi, M., (1990), *Flow: The Psychology of Optimal Experience,* Harper and Row, New York.

Ganim, B., and Fox, S. (1999), *Visual Journaling: Going Deeper than Words*, Quest Books, Wheaton, Illinois.

Glasser, W. (1985), *Control Theory: A New Explanation of How We Control our Lives*, Harper & Row, New York.

Katie, B. (2000), *Loving What Is: Four Questions that can Change your Life,* Rider, London.

Krishnamurti, J. (1991), *The Awakening of Intelligence*, Victor Gollancz Ltd., London.

Maslow, A.H. (1943), 'A Theory of Human Motivation', in Psychological Review, 50(4), 370–96.

Tolle, E. (1999), *The Power of Now: A Guide to Spiritual Enlightenment,* New World Library, California.

10830663R00072